JACE STEPS UP
TO DAILY TASKS

WRITTEN BY JACE PERRY AND SABRINA WILSON

Jace Steps Up

Copyright © 2024 Sabrina Wilson

All rights reserved. No part of this publication may be reproduced, distributed, or transmitted in any form or by any means, including photocopying, recording, or other electronic or mechanical methods, without the prior written permission of the publisher.

Revolt Renaissance Publishing

Library of Congress Control Number: 2024918750

Hi, I'm Jace! I am nine years old. I have dwarfism. This means my arms and legs are shorter than most children my age. My little brother Jaxon who is six, is much taller than me. That doesn't stop me from helping him as much as I can. I also have a baby brother named Ellis. We are the same height even though he's two. That doesn't stop me from taking care of him.

My big sister, Emirie, is eleven, and my older brother, Julius, is sixteen.

We are always excited to complete our morning tasks and head to school.

It's not always as easy for me to get ready as it is for my siblings.

I sometimes need a little help from my stool, but I know my superpower comes from my ability to think big. I may be small, but I can conquer the world!

It's morning, and it's time for me to prepare for school.

Fun fact:

October is Dwarfism Awareness Month.

First, I must wash my face and brush my teeth. Oh no! I can't reach the sink! What should I do? I know! I can get my step stool to reach the sink.

Fun fact:

A person with dwarfism is usually 4'10 and under.

Yay! I did it! My stool always comes in handy when it comes to helping me complete my daily tasks. My face and teeth are all nice and clean.

Fun fact:

Jace is an achondroplasia dwarf.

Next, I go and make my bed. Oh no! I forgot my stool in the bathroom! I always need my stool to help make my bed neat.

Fun fact:

Did you know that there are 200 different types of dwarfism?

I grab my stool and step up to my bed so my covers are nice and tidy. My stool is always so helpful when it comes to helping me complete my daily tasks. Yay! I did it! My bed looks great.

Fun fact:

Did you know that for every 1 out of 10,000 births, a child with dwarfism is born?

Then, I pick out my clothes for school. Oh no! My shirts are at the top of my dresser. My mom must have mistakenly put them there. She usually places them down at the bottom so I can reach them. It's so much easier for me when things are lower, but it's OK. I know what I should do.

Fun fact:

Many dwarfs would prefer to be called little people or called by their names.

I'll grab my stool to help me reach my shirts. Yay! I got it.

Fun fact:

Did you know that only 30,000 people in America have dwarfism?

My stool always helps me step up to get things that are out of reach. I am done putting on my clothes. I look handsome!

Fun fact:

Did you know that dwarfism occurs equally across all racial and ethnic groups?

Last but not least, it's time for me to make myself some breakfast. I love toaster strudels. I'll grab some from the freezer! Now I need to heat them. Oh no! The toaster is on top of the counter. What should I do? I know! I should grab my step stool to reach the toaster.

Fun fact:

Did you know that people with dwarfism often have average-sized organs?

Yay! I did it! My step stool always helps me complete my daily tasks. My strudels are delicious.

Fun fact:

It is rare to have any mental cognition issues in conjunction with dwarfism.

Finally, I am ready to go to school. It's time for me to get into the car. Oh no! The car door handles are way too high. What should I do? I know! I should grab my stool that I keep in the garage. My stool always helps me reach things that are too high.

Fun fact:

There are athletes with dwarfism who compete in the Paralympic Games.

Yay! I did it. Off to school. I thank Yah for my step stool. It always helps me complete my daily tasks. I can step up to anything. I can conquer being small with help from my step stool.

Fun fact:

80% of people with dwarfism have average height parents.

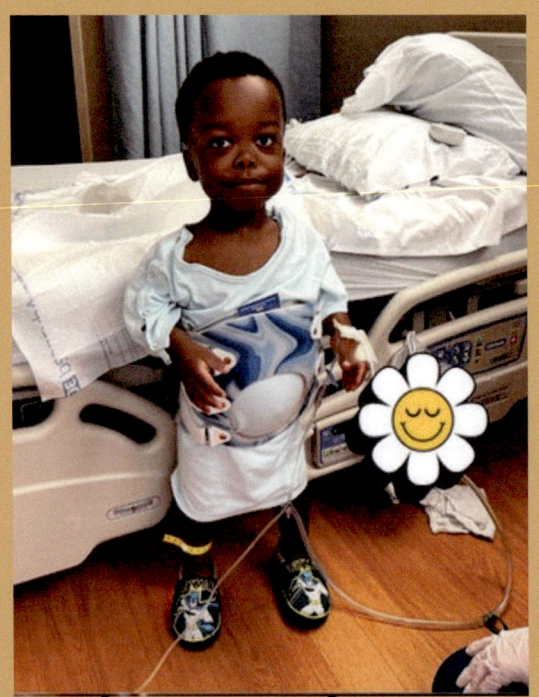

Jace's X-ray images before and after spine repair and infusion.

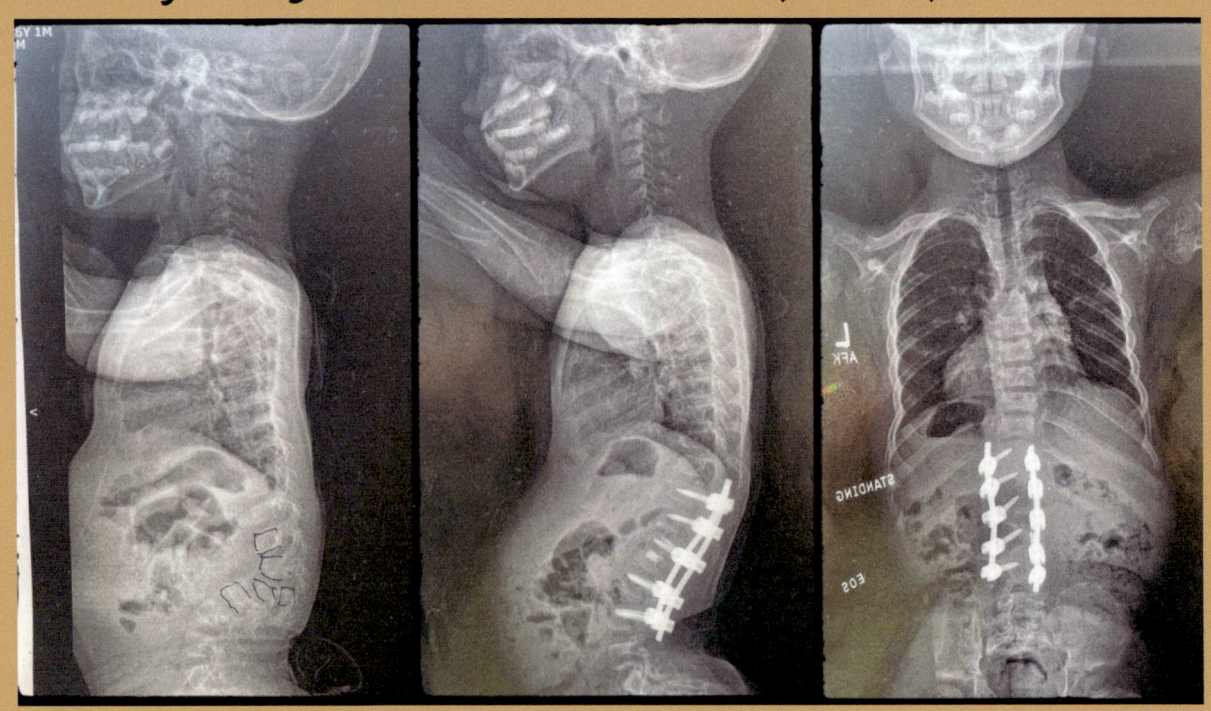

Jace Perry is a nine-year-old achondroplasia dwarf. Jace's parents were not aware of his diagnosis during pregnancy, and his dwarfism came as a complete surprise.

Although the doctor didn't detect Jace's dwarfism condition, and it came as a big surprise to the family, Jace was such a rare blessing to their lives.

Jace has grown up to be a loving, happy, brave, wise, and intelligent young man. He knows how to bring life to the room. He is a joy to be around and enjoys spending time with friends and family.

Most people are unaware that when little people are born, they are diagnosed with other medical issues. Jace was diagnosed with one of the most common disorders for most achondroplasia dwarfs, which is scoliosis.

Jace lived and thrived with scoliosis, playing and having fun with his siblings until around age six. Severe back pains began, but God blessed the family with the talented Dr. David Bumpass, who repaired Jace's spine and helped him get out of pain. Jace healed so fast! Everyone was so astonished by the way Jace recovered with no back pains.

Although Jace may have been born with a condition he can't control, he is a warrior, full of charisma, and has much to offer to the world.

Printed by Libri Plureos GmbH in Hamburg, Germany